A Match Made in Heaven

How to Marry Your Vocation to Your Divine Calling

———————

Catherine E. Storing

A Match Made in Heaven

Published in the United States by Writing Made Simple Books, Boston MA

A Match Made in Heaven: How to Marry Your Vocation to Your Divine Calling
Copyright © 2017 All rights reserved.

No part of this book may be reproduced, stored, in a retrieval system, or transmitted by any means, electronic, mechanical, photocopying, recording, or otherwise, without written permission from the copyright holder.
For any ordering information or special discounts for bulk purchases, please contact Writing Made Simple at catherine@catherinestoring.com

Match Made in Heaven:
How to Marry Your Vocation to Your Divine Calling
Copyright © 2017 All rights reserved.

By Writing Made Simple Publishing

All rights reserved. No part of this book may be reproduced or transmitted in any form or by any means without permission from the author.

ISBN-194-1-253601
ISBN13- 978-1-941253-60-1

Printed in USA

Also by Catherine E. Storing

1. Dream Big: Seven Keys to Stepping Into Your Calling
2. Soñando en Mayuscula: Siete Claves para Alcanzar tu Vocacion
3. Styling Faith: The Complete Style Guide
4. Confidence: 8 Bold Steps to Arrive to Your Calling in Style
5. Relationships: Dress and Date Like You Have Inside Information
6. La Pareja Ideal: Vistete Como si Tuvieras Informacion Privilegiada
7. From Dream to Destiny: Unlocking The Winner, Champion, and the Finisher Within
8. The Confidence to Wait: How to Cleverly and Biblically Answer to Others and Yourself: "Why are YOU Still Single?"
9. The Conversations (Novel coming out in 2017)

A Match Made in Heaven

I have a FREE gift for you. I recorded a Master Class JUST for you! This Master Class will help you not only to find your calling but to also FINALLY accept it.

Request your FREE Master Class here: http://bit.ly/ammihbook-giveaway

My gift to you,

Catherine E. Storing

Dedication

I dedicate this book to EVERY creative person who desires to share their gifts and talents with the world in ways that brings honor to God.

Table of Contents

Forward 10

Introduction 12

Chapter 1 29

Chapter 2 43

Chapter 3 52

Chapter 4 65

Chapter 5 75

Chapter 6 85

Chapter 7 98

Chapter 8 107

Chapter 9 122

Chapter 10 127

Conclusion 131

About the Author 136

Gift 138

Forward

There are certain people who God ordains to be conversations starters. Just like God appointed Jeremiah to be a prophet unto the nations before he was formed inside of his mother's womb, there are those who are slated to initiate specific conversations that create openings for particular shifts to occur in the earth realm.

I believe Catherine Storing to be one of those individuals who God created to be a conversation starter. In her book, A Match Made In Heaven, she initiates a conversation that has been rehearsed in the minds of many who are highly anointed in ministry and the marketplace. This book is the answer for those who are endeavoring to show up in the world as the best version of themselves; in the duality of their vocation and their call.

Catherine Storing is an expert in this area because she is the epitome of obedience to both the call and vocation. I have heard Catherine say on numerous occasions, "I can do it all, and I don't have to choose!" Her words have blazed a trail for those of us who have the same sentiment. Reading this book will empower you with the reality that you too… "Don't have to choose!"

Pastor Kimberly Jones M.A., CMLC
Living on Purpose Life & Empowerment Coaching
CEO/Founder

Introduction

I am so excited to share this content with you today. Did you know that it was hard for me to get to this place? I am not talking about physically; I am speaking spiritually. It took me 40 years to get here. Today is a brand-new day! As I write this, I am celebrating my 41st birthday, but today is also a celebration of so many things that I've been dying to share with others.

Let me explain, for the last couple of years maybe for more than that I have been struggling to find balance and I just could not. Has that ever happened to you? You know you are way off but have NO idea how to find balance? That was me. I was really on fire in my faith and my business, but I made a concerted effort to keep both separate, like church and state. However, that solution was not working for me. Both left me feeling unfulfilled like I was missing something, but I had no idea what that something was.

Since April 30th of 2017, big things have been happening, and God has been putting them together, but at the same time, He has not been in a big hurry either. Have you ever felt that GOD was taking His sweet time to bless you and deliver you? Well, that is what has been happening to me.

Just this last Monday, He put something together in an excellent way, and all I could say was:

"Did You just do that in an awesome, awesome way?" To which He responded.

"Yeah, that is what I do." That's my Daddy, that's why I love Him so much. He loves me in so many surprising ways.

Before I continue sharing how awesome the God we serve is and how He showed me the marvelous way to balance it all, can we take a moment to pray?

[Prayer]

Heavenly Father, You are so amazing, I cannot think of a better way; I cannot think of a better place, I cannot think of other readers to share and celebrate the day that you decided I would be born…again.

Father God, this is the day You ordained for me to do what You have created me to do. There are so many attached to the woman you created me to be, perfectly imperfect for these people. There are readers all over the world that were predestined to read this, to be in this atmosphere, to understand exactly what you have prepared for them. I pray that You open minds, that you open hearts, that you open ears and that anything that stands in the way for them receiving this amazing Word you have prepared for them, not because I'm delivering it, but because You prepared it because You decided that today was the day.

Father, give me the anointing, give me the wisdom, and just give me joy as I share what you have deposited in my heart. This is so amazing! It is such a gift. I do not take it lightly; I do not take lightly this privilege to be able to share what You have put in my heart. This comes from You. Therefore, I thank You in advance for the amazing things we are going to experience throughout this book, and I pray that You help me to deliver this in a concise and clear way. I am well aware of my long-winded tendencies but Father, you can do Above and beyond what we can think or imagine so I know there is hope for me yet.

Thank you, Father! We are NOT in a hurry, so we are more than willing to listen from you, knowing that is going to take as long as it needs to take. We have wasted so much time doing other foolish things that we are not going to put a limit to the blessings. You want to gift us with today.

Thank You in advance for being awesome, amazing, and we cannot wait to see what You are going to do. We ask for ALL these things with high expectations. We asked for this with the highest of expectations, and we say thank You in the most precious and most Holy name, the Name of Jesus. Amen and amen!

As I said earlier, I wrote this content on my actual birthday, and I knew it was going to be a special day; I knew the day was going to be different. I have known that for months now. I remember saying to God:

"God, what's going to happen in May?" May has always been a month of new beginnings for me. This was more of a rhetorical question I needed no actual answer.

I ALREADY knew it was going to be different. I knew that something was going to happen just by seeing what God had been doing in my life so far.

Take for instance December - that's when I was trying to promote one of my courses Write Like A Pro, but I did not feel at liberty to so because God said it wasn't time yet. And since He said so, I did not do it. I was not about to become a disobedient daughter…anymore.

I had no choice but to wait for Him to tell me what He wanted me to do. And I did not have to wait long, December 10th, 2016 came around like any other ordinary day, but He had something pretty awesome for me.

On December 10th, my friends and spiritual leaders Apostle Louis Jones and his wife, Pastor Kimberly Jones had an overnight prayer service at Prevailing Love Worship Center in Stone Mountain Georgia, and it was incredible. It was life changing.

I was able to participate in the prayer service because they were kind enough to broadcast the event via Periscope – a LIVE streaming app that may or may not is active still by the time you read this book – anyway I watched not knowing God would be speaking to me that night.

2016 was a tough year for me. I don't know how it was for you but for me, 2016 beat me up for real, like 2016 just got my number, and it just wouldn't let go. I got more beatings than a tambourine at a Pentecostal service. By the time December came around, I was more than excited. I said to myself:

"Okay, December is here! That means that 2017 is just around the corner and I KNOW that will be my year of new beginnings. The nonsense, spiritual and emotional beatings will go away."

God did not disappoint, during that service God used both Apostle and Pastor Kimberly – PK for short – to share some words of encouragement with me. And them words were right on time, like salve to my wounds. What did I do with it? The nerdy part me did the following:

1. Downloaded the Periscope video
2. Converted the video to an MP3 file
3. Found the four minutes of prophecy and trimmed off the rest of the video
4. Uploaded that short MP3 file to my beloved iPhone

Yeap I did ALL that, I may not wear plaid shirts or have a pocket protector, but I'm a total geek. I love me some technology.

Since I added that short clip to my phone months ago I forget it's even there; I have all kinds of praise songs and audio clips there too, so when I listen to music the clip comes up 'randomly.' The funny thing is that it ONLY comes up 'randomly' when I need it or when I am feeling a little lost.

The words Apostle first spoke to me sounded kind of lovely at first, I mean He was so happy to share them with me that I was excited too. But then I found myself saying:

"I don't know about that; I don't know what he is talking about'.

But God had a purpose. If God had shown me what He meant back on December 10, 2016, I wouldn't have been able to receive it. The old me couldn't receive that. I just couldn't see it.

I'll tell you in a minute what He said and how God put it together in an amazing way, but I just wanted to set the stage so I could show you how God has been putting this thing together piece by piece.

I'm always in the middle of either writing a book or finishing a book. There is no in-between. I think at the moment I'm on book number thirteen or fourteen. But guess what? My Books to write file on Evernote – a fantastic app EVERY writer should use - I have about forty-five titles of books God has put a burden on my heart to write.

Writing is what God has called me to do. He has even shown me someone that has written MANY more books than the number of books He has called me to write. It's almost as if He were saying:

"That thing I called you to do is not as impossible as you may think it is." God is awesome like that, He gives you a BIG calling, but then He shows you a brief preview to encourage you.

Do you know who John Maxwell is? He is a fantastic Business and faith-based leader in the Atlanta area; he has written hundreds of books. As much as I love his LIVE teachings, I do not enjoy listening to his audiobooks. One day, I'll meet him and will get to tell him:

"I like your sermons and live teachings; it would be so great if your audio books reflected that candidness your readers have come to trust and love." I will tell him that. But I digress…let's get on with the story. I went to his website one day, and I saw pages upon pages, book after book, and I said to myself:

"One day I will have a page similar to this on my website. It will never be about the quantity, but about the hope, and encouragement those books will be for others." And that was that. I quickly forgot about the episode. Please know that I do not want to be John Maxwell; I want to write the number of books God has called me to write, but I do love what I saw, what is possible.

And then something amazing happened last year, I wrote my first novel. Can I tell you that it took me a long time to write that book? It took me TWENTY years to write and finish my first book, even though I have been a writer nearly my entire life. My Spanish writing game was strong; I was prolific. God gave me that gift. It is a gift that He has given me- I used to write plays, and poetry like nobody's business.

Unfortunately, or just like God planned before the beginning of time my entire family moved to the US right after I completed high school. You won't believe what happened? I lost my writing voice; that thing that used to wake me up in the middle of the night with stories, verses, and rhymes

I thought I missed the gift forever; I just couldn't do it. Every time I tried, the enemy would tell me I was not good enough, things like:

"How are you going to write at the level you used to write before or even better?" Sadly, I believed that BIG fat lies for a very long time.

A couple of years ago before my thirty-ninth birthday, I said to God:

"God, I cannot have another year of this. God, this is not right. I need help." I knew that ALL I needed was to see that it was possible. I needed to finish the first book. I got some help. And guess what? I wrote my first short book in JUST eight hours.

Just as I predicted I have not stopped writing, I LITERALLY cannot stop. I found my writing voice again. I was so happy to be writing again that I thought that was it, the end of the blessing.

"I found my voice! This is amazing! I'm ready to go." But God had a different plan for my life. He had a bigger plan for me.

Yes, that was a LOT of background, but it is SO essential for the journey we are about to embark on together. You picked up this book because you desperately want to know how to stop splitting or compartmentalizing your life. Keep reading and allow God to use my story and life experiences to shed light on your own story and life experiences.

He has been weaving a beautiful life, equipping you along the way, I know that may not make much sense to you since all you can probably see is the pain, heartache, and loss. But please know that in between all of that, God was depositing blessings that have been gaining compound interest in your life. Just keep reading and allow God to show you what He has been up to in your life.

Allow me to confess to you that I have been struggling with the same issue for five years?

For five years I have yo-yo-ed between the faith-only corner and then all the way to the opposite business-only corner. I just could not find the balance I was talking about earlier.

Out of sheer desperation, I asked the Father to show me what the issue was, and He in His infinite mercy showed me with an illustration. He knows me so well; stories are my favorite way to learn.

"Catherine, what you are doing is as if you would have taken a car that was meant to be driven, cut that car in half and now you are behind that car pushing it with your bare-arms, and you are wondering why you are not moving faster.

You have taken something that I created to be leveraged together, you have separated it, and you are wondering why is not working as I told you it would. You are wondering why it is not moving at speed you know it's capable of achieving." What He said made total sense to me. Let me tell you how I was feeling at the time. It was as if I had taken too many allergy pills and my body was awake but lethargic. I wanted to move fast, run even but it just could not.

Again, I pleaded with God:

"God, I am grinding and grinding, and things are not moving at speed I know possible." I was so frustrated because I knew what God said. He said I could do this. He had given me the resources, the know-how, the desire to work, and still, it wasn't working.

I thought – and this is where you have to be VERY careful when you ask God to tell people to do something about a problem you are experiencing or see others experiencing – this is what I said:

"Somebody should write a book about how they were able to successfully merge their vocation to their calling." I was feeling so good about myself; I told God about a need I was experiencing, and I was sure He would assign someone to jump on it the right way.

"You are somebody, so maybe you should take care of that." When God speaks you move so this is the reason why I HAD to write this book, I truly had no choice but to write it for me first and then for you. I hope this book blesses you as much as it has blessed me.

A Match Made in Heaven

Chapter One
It Was Not Random

Everything - I mean EVERYTHING - will be used - is of use - for what which YOU have been called to do.

I can feel your eyes getting bigger and your protests building up but before you go losing your marbles on me let me give you some examples:

1. Upbringing
2. Relationships (the good, the bad, and the not so great ones).
3. Jobs (with a big capital "S" because just like you I have had EVERY job you can think of; I know PK, and I have that in common). The jobs did not have ANYTHING in common – other than me – Yes, we did well at probably all of those jobs, but that was not what we were called to do.
4. Doors (opened and closed doors)
5. Successes

6. Losses
7. Training
8. Connections
9. Rejections

I worked in corporate America for seventeen years, this what I always say about that VERY dark period of my life:

"I got out early for good behavior." The last position I held was killing me; it was a prolonged death – like a rotisserie chicken slowly cooking from the inside out –

I was there for FOUR long years I could not help myself, so I asked my Daddy: "God, why am I still here? I am so sick of this! I cannot take this anymore! I was not created to sit at a desk writing email after email about nonsense, and going to meeting after meeting that was about yet another inconsequential meeting."

I recall leaving those meetings, and LITERALLY, nothing was accomplished. And the worse part, I would have to do that again the following week, the week after that and even more heartbreaking, the week after that.

If it is your desire to kill me quickly just make me sit in a meeting about a meeting where people don't want to be. And to put the final nail in the coffin make sure none of the attendees get any of the assigned work completed.

Resulting yet in another meeting where hopefully Johnny would do the assignment.

However, at the next meeting, Johnny would have a barrage of excuses like:

"What had happened was..." "I got started, but Stephanie did not send her reports in on time…" "I thought this meeting got canceled." "My dog died..." Blah blah blah he would go on avoiding getting any actual work done.

And just like that, I sat in that miserable existence for seventeen years, and I was R E S E N T F U L.

Can you tell I had a stinking attitude? I had a brown girl attitude about that job. I hated all the jobs that came before that one too, but that last one I just could not do anymore. I couldn't take it anymore; I was so sick of it, SO tired of it.

Did you know that God did not release me from that job until I got EVERY bit of training I needed for the Kingdom?

They paid for ALL the training; they trained me so well that I went from – let me interject here for a second and point out that I'm smart. I am VEY smart, but I wasn't numbers smart. I could do numbers, but I was not analytical. I even used to say that about myself. "I'm not analytical." Have you ever said similar things about yourself?

"I'm not this!" "I'm not analytical." "I'm not an author." Or my ultimate favorite: "It's going to take me a long time to finish this or that."

And you say that thing over and over about yourself, and then God has to work in you until you stop saying those lies about yourself. Finally, God had to say to me:

"There is no deficiency in what I created. Do you mean that I made you deficient? Are you saying that I did not put in you everything that you needed to do what I have called you to do?" He said in His thunderous voice. That voice He uses when He means business. He did not release me from that job until Catherine Storing was A N A L Y T I C A L.

Can I tell you that I can analyze ANYTHING? I can look at numbers and see patterns. ME! This girl right here. I have always been all about the words; I am all about dictionaries; I'm all about beautiful looking paragraphs. Still, He did not release me from that job until I was able to realize that I could be analytical.

He fixed my mindset about numbers all right, but that was not ALL He needed to change while I was still working 'for the man.'

Conflict used to be a FOUR-letter word for yours truly. I would avoid it like the plague. I didn't know how to put people in their place in a nice way. I didn't want to tell people "Hey, you are stepping on my toes," or "Listen, I don't like what you are saying about me."

What did God do? He continued to put these difficult/hard-to-love people in my life until I had no recourse but to say to someone, "Listen, that's not cool!" without losing my peace either; staying calm and collected, without remaining hostage of anger and frustration.

So, it wasn't random. ALL them situations were shaping me, shaving off, molding and reallocating resources/thoughts into the right place. I want you to do something for me, think about:

    a. All the situations
    b. Marriages
    c. Miscarriages
    d. Fights

e. Abuse, etc.

All that stuff, meditate on how they played a part in your re-education.

Make a list of all the things you have gone through (need help? Look at the categories mentioned above, they should get you started) and look back and say, "What did God try to show me there? What skill, gift did I have to refine in that season?"

_____

_____

_____

_____

_____

_____

_____

_____

_____

_____

A Match Made in Heaven

A Match Made in Heaven

A Match Made in Heaven

_____
_____
_____
_____
_____
_____
_____
_____
_____
_____
_____
_____
_____
_____
_____
_____

Maybe you are fighting off something right now, I can only guess, after all I don't know you like that, but maybe there is something you are struggling with in your life.

Can I tell you what the Father has said to me in those moments?

"Honey/Darling, do you know that I mean this for good and not evil, right? You know I sent that annoying person, or neighbor to teach you a lesson, right?"

Sometimes it is a relative, someone you share the same last name with, somebody you cannot divorce, or you cannot leave behind. God uses that person, and in the flesh, you feel like saying: (I know because I have done it, MANY times).

"This moment, again. I'm done!!! I'm never going to see you again!" But in those moments God would say:

"That's not what I want you to do because if you JUST get along with the people who are easy to get along with, where is the growth in that? Anybody can do that! Even the Gentiles can do that, but you, Honey, need to learn how to love hard people to love. Do you know why? As delightful as you are, and as impressive as those red curls are, YOU are NOT easy to love either."

I know I'm not as easy to love as I thought at first because He has shown me the way He wants me to go and I fight Him. It might be effortless for us to say:

"That person is so hard to love." But if we stop for a moment and ask an even better question: "what about me, am I easy to love by the Father?"

Let's look at this when God shows us the way to go, but we do not listen and become hard headed, we are JUST like that person in our lives we find hard to love.

Do you know how hard that is to hear? Do you know how hard that is to accept, that you are just as hard to love as that person you can't stand?

Doesn't that help you a little bit to love that person a bit more? Doesn't that help you to put yourself in their shoes and realize that there are moments when you can be hard headed? There are moments when you can be hard to love too.

And then you must accept that the situation or difficulty you are fighting, that thing you no longer want in your life is the VERY thing God is using to deliver you.

But what if you asked a different question:

"how can I look at this the way my Daddy means it for me?" The moment you do that you change your perspective about that thing, you are set free.

The moment you are free, peace is going to wash over you like nobody's business. You realize you just needed to let go. You just needed to see it the way your Daddy sees it. If you do that in every area of your life, you think is random your life will change.

Our Daddy is not random. He is SO on-purpose; He doesn't waste a second. So, when you get passed on for a job promotion when you get delayed because you can't find parking, the business is not taking off, or when somebody gossips about you, I want you to ask yourself this question:

"What is God trying to show me?" Remember, He is not pushing you out. He has not forgotten about you. He loves you so much that He has put that situation right in front of you to deliver you. It's not random!

Chapter Two
Adjust Your Expectations

Stop assuming - Not everything that comes to you is permanent or temporary - there is no precedent to what your life will be. You are on a path unique to you. The trip will be smoother when you lose your grip on what you think your life should be.

How many times do we lose our temper over things that are temporary and should not matter? Too many times to count I am sure, at least that's true for me.

We act like it is the end of the world as if we were going to deal with that situation forever?

Let me share a perfect example, I was at a job for four years, JUST four years, and to me, it felt like an eternity. Four years is NOTHING! Let's compare that to the time I have spent on earth, forty-one years.

How about we review this job I hated so much?

a. Eight weeks paid vacation
b. Base Salary: over $100,000/year
c. Five minutes from my house
d. Tons of schedule flexibility
e. Performance based bonus
f. Major holidays off
g. Top notch health care coverage
h. And a bunch of other perks I can't even recall right now.

I can almost hear your voice screaming: "Come on, Catherine! Really? And you acted like you were working in a sweatshop."

Not only did I enjoy ALL them benefits, but they were also training me as well. I could argue that it was not the right way to train me, but still, I learned a valuable lesson: when things are done the wrong way they still teach us great lessons, probably even more memorable ones than the well-taught lessons.

Case in point, my last boss, taught me the most, he managed me so poorly that I can't help but to remember.

What did that too for me? It set me up to become the best boss I could be. I'm going to manage people the right way, and I will encourage them EVERY step of the way.

My old boss taught me; he helped me, even now he is still teaching me. His attitude was wrong, so what? He taught me. He didn't know the best way to say things, but he taught me, so what?

One day, I'll see him, and I'll be able to say: "Listen I'm sorry I had such a stinking attitude when I used to work for you. I should have left the job earlier if my heart was no longer in it; you were doing the best you could. Thank you for everything.

Stop assuming that everything that is happening in your life is permanent or that is not for your good.

Are you one of those people that when they are going through something amazing cannot help but lament: "Oh, I know this is not going to last, at any moment the car will breakdown, or someone will get sick. I just know it."

Statements like that make my blood boil. Why question the blessing? Why go to the negative instead of enjoying the blessing from the Lord?

I wish it just stopped there; we even go as far as to declare:

"I'm going to get sick." "I'm going to get fired."

Many are so consumed with their negative mindset that they don't even get to enjoy the blessing because they are always thinking about the next thing that might go wrong.

You need to stop assuming things. I can tell you that there's no precedent for your life. You are walking a path that nobody has EVER walked before.

Some people might be wondering:
"Why is she not doing that, like little Susie over there?" When others around you say things like that to you, they tend to catch you off guard, and for a brief moment, you entertained the thought too.

"Why am I NOT doing things like little Susie? Why am I not doing my business the way she's doing it?"
At that moment, you don't even know how to respond because you are thinking the same thing they are thinking.

But God is so awesome He wants to whisper to you when you are FINALLY in the safety of your own home - make the time to get in the Word and pray:

"Honey, you are NOT like little Susie. You are unique. I have a path for you that makes no sense to the natural mind. It's going to be like this a while longer, but in the end, it turns out better than okay. Trust me."

Have you seen people paint prophetically? The entire process looks random, a dab of paint over here and a dab of paint over there. It sounds like a hot mess, but then they step back, and you see the complete picture, and it makes perfect sense.

Little Susie's path, it's for Susie. Her way is simple; anybody can see where it will lead. That's for her, that's why is simple. That's why she is already there, and that's what she can handle.

Are you getting it now? Your path/calling is so much more complicated because He has predestined a bigger blessing for you. He has so much more for you than you can imagine. Let them say whatever they are going to say about your calling.

In the end, it will be their turn to step back and look at ALL the ways God used you mightily for His glory. In the end, they will see how there were so many turns here and there, but He is the ultimate authority when it comes to your future. Remember, He is already there; He has seen your future. He knows how it ends. It is good. A perfect ending indeed.

I have always wanted to take crew lessons, I knew it would be fun, but I did not know it would change my life in so many ways. I got to do just that earlier in the month.

For example, the first week is, we were having some issues with grasping our oars. Let me stop for a moment to tell you that crew oars are NOT like regular oars. For starters, crew oars are about six feet long, and we have to row backward, so roars don't see where they are going or what's coming up.

Good thing we can count on the person in front of us, telling us what to do, he or she can see what's going on because they have a better view of what's ahead.

God is trustworthy and is in control of everything. He is aware of what is going to happen because even BEFORE He put us together in our mother's womb He already knew all about our future.

So who cares if things don't look like they are going to work out? What if your brother's or your cousin's life look WAY better than your own at this moment? This is not the end. God is putting the final touches, and when YOU step back you will see, you will see what He prepared for you. It'll be worth the wait. Worth anything and everything the enemy throws your way.

So yeah, it was not random. He has it ALL under control and will use it for His glory and your good.

Take hold of this promise:

For I know the plans and thoughts that I have for you,' says the LORD, 'plans for peace and well-being and not for disaster, to give you a future and a hope.
Jeremiah 29:11 AMP

Chapter Three
Stay Connected And Don't Let Go

Let me ask you something, have you ever gone through something difficult and decided to just take a break from everything? I know I have. Plenty of times I have chosen to go to my little corner to pray and 'dealt' with the problem all by myself.

What about taking a break from your friends all together? After that got old, you probably decided to take a break from even praying, and that's when the enemy attacked you, was not it? Why? Because in moments like that is when you need someone to remind you what God says about you, about all the blessings He has in store for you.

What do we do when the going gets tough? We let go because it's so scary because when the boat starts shaking the natural response is to want to get out.

Many times, we are the ones that make the boat we call life rock back and forth like crazy. How? When we are out sync with God. In those moments, we choose to get ahead of His plan for us. I have done that myself SO many times I have lost count. The good thing about that is that I am FINALLY learning to recognize when I am in those seasons, so I now slow down or stop altogether.

What does God want us to do when life, work, our health or anything we care about is out of control, and we don't know what to do? Just stay in the exact place He told you to be. Don't let go of your position. If He asked you to be there, that is where you need to be. There's no other place for you to be. Stay there until He says: 'move!'

In those situations, is when you need to be the most connected spiritually. What situations am I talking about? For example, when for no reason at all people start jumping at you with attacks, insults, and unreasonable demands. Those are the moments you have to press on. You might say things like:

"I am not going to get up, I'm so tired," you lament. Why? Because you stayed up for most of the night worrying. Have you ever done that? What have we ever accomplished by worrying? In the history of time, have we ever accomplished anything by wasting our time thinking about the-what if scenarios we indulge in? We have achieved zero!

The not so funny thing is that most of the time in the morning when you get up then the problem is not even there anymore.

What did you gain? Just wasted precious moments worrying and complaining. What could you have done instead? You could have stayed connected to Him.

Don't let go of your prayer time; don't let go of your Bible time; don't let go of praying for other people either.

How many times do you just pray for you, you, and oh yes, you? While many people go through even worse calamities than what you are going through. Quit acting like you are the ONLY person going through a rough season and start praying like the mighty warrior you were created to be.

The Real Purpose of Trials

Have you ever stop to think the reason why God allows attacks and lack in your life? You must have thought about it. After all, God does not waste an opportunity to get us closer to Him, right? I have come to realize that EVERYTHING that has happened to be had a purpose, a particular purpose.

After I stopped my whining and complaining and to be honest, forgot about that issue or attack, God would remind me of the lessons I learned during a particular season. I would then realize that without that season I would not have the skills to either minister to someone or to get through a new rough season.

EVERYTHING works together for good to those who love Him and are called according to His will right? We learn that in Romans 8:28. That scripture gets quoted a lot but have you ever taken the time to think about it? Let's examine it a little deeper – by now you know I am partial to the Bible's amplified version, right? Good.

"And we know [with great confidence]"

Do you know? Really? I love how Paul makes it a statement: "And we know." The apostle did not guess, he knew.

Next time you are going through something remember this comforting truth. He is working it all out. EVERYTHING.

"That God [who is deeply concerned about us]"

How awesome is that? I think it's amazing. Who are we for God to care that much for us? I don't think I will ever understand why but I am sure grateful that He cares even about minute details of our lives. Remember that even when small stuff is happening and you think it has NOTHING to do with your calling. In the end, it will come together rather nicely. Just remember that.

"causes all things to work together [as a plan]"

Remember the last chapter when we talked about the plan He has for us? This is just another reminder for you, God is already in our future, even before we were born, so remember: He has orchestrated EVERYTHING about you. He has an excellent plan. I love that about God. He does not leave anything to happenstance; no, He takes advantage of our mistakes, especially our arrogant disobedience. Aren't you thankful for that? How did He know you would act like a rebellious and stubborn two-year old and still He chose to use that nasty attitude and behavior? I most certainly am.

"for good for those who love God."

Many people like to quote the first part of this verse and very often forget about this part, probably the most important part. Don't kid yourself, NOT everything that happens to everyone works out for good. That little caveat is reserved for His children. The ones that in spite of their crazy behavior and constant disregard for God's statutes still love Him. Is that you? Are you one of the few that love Him? If you are not, you are missing out BIG time.

Loving God is one of the best decisions you will ever make in your life. And not because of all the perks – and there are many – but because loving Him and being close to Him are the best parts of being alive. Experiencing His love in a world lost, and without hope, it really is what makes many of us get up in the morning and face yet again evil, disappointment, injustice, and heartbreak.

His love is the driving force behind everything those who love Him do and live for.

"to those who are called"

This is the part where you come in, are you called? Well, are you? To be fair, you may not even know. This is how you know you were called: you are breathing. I know, it may sound corny but is true.

God does not waste ANYTHING, especially time. He took the time to put you together; He gave you gifts and talents. What are those? Those abilities you take for granted, like decorating, friendliness, writing or praying for others. I could spend hours listing ALL the gifts you were given.

Those gifts were given to you on loan, for you to use well until His return. You will have to give an account of how you used your gifts as Jesus explained in the parable of the talents in Luke 19. Read it when you have a moment, but for now, let me share this section with you:

[Jesus explained,] 'I tell you that to everyone who has [because he valued his gifts from God and has used them wisely], more will be given; but from the one who does not have [because he disregarded his gifts from God], even what he has will be taken away.'
Luke 19:26 AMP

You, my friend, possess MANY MANY gifts sitting stagnant somewhere, collecting dust while many people go without because of your disobedience. Don't neglect Jesus's warning about gifts being take away because of misusage or lack of use.

"according to His plan and purpose."

The key word above is 'His.' It is NOT according to our plan or purpose. I know it would be so great if it were but actually, it would not. We have proven that theory wrong every time we have tried to take over. We failed miserably EVERY single time.

His plan and purpose, He does not do things just because, no He has a purpose and that purpose, in the end, is ALWAYS good for us. Never forget that. Okay? Good.

Now that we are clear on that let us do a quick gifts/talents inventory. (Think about ALL the things you are able to do better and easier than anybody else. What do people say you are great all the time?)

_____

_____

_____

_____

_____

_____

_____

_____

A Match Made in Heaven

A Match Made in Heaven

There is a FREE resource I have used before that you might like. You can find it here:

https://www.lifeway.com/lwc/files/lwcF_PDF_Discover_Your_Spiritual_Gifts.pdf

Chapter Four
Listen - Everything is Speaking to You

Listening requires you to rest, to be still and clear your mind. If you are too busy and too stimulated, you will continue to miss all the clues and directions God is sending your way. When I talk about over-stimulated, I'm talking about your boyfriend or your lover. You know whom I'm talking about, right? Sometimes, your phone, at times it's Facebook, Twitter, Instagram, any device; your iPad, or your laptop.

I don't know what your vice is. Maybe you still have a blackberry or a beeper (younger folks, those were electronic devices before we had the gift of iPhones).

Whatever it is, one thing is clear; it is closer to you than God is to you.

Think about before you go to bed when you have one spare second; your hands are always going to it; whether listening or looking, you don't have one moment of down time.

The funny thing is that then you wonder why when you go to church or sit down to pray your mind starts to attack you. Has that ever happened to you? Lots of ideas coming at you faster than you can process. You even say to yourself:

"Whoa, what is going on here? Give me a break, brain please!" But your mind says:

"Hold on? You just stopped for five minutes. This is the only time we have; let's give you all the thoughts we have been trying to share with you."

You need down time; you need a brain break. You need that daily. Your device should not be the first thing you pick up in the morning or when you have free time. It cannot be the last thing either because God loves to use dreams to talk to you. Allow your mind a few minutes of downtime or rest before you fall to sleep, and you are more than likely to notice more restful nights.

Are you a news-watching person? I have not watched the news in ages. "Wow I feel so inspired, and my faith in humanity has been renewed." Said no one after watching the news. I know that many things are happening in the media, especially politically but let me tell you, there will always be negative campaigns and people committing heinous crimes, don't allow yourself to be consumed by all of that. Instead do as the apostle said in Philippians 4:8 AMP

> *Finally, believers, whatever is true, whatever is honorable and worthy of respect, whatever is right and confirmed by God's word, whatever is pure and wholesome, whatever is lovely and brings peace, whatever is admirable and of good repute; if there is any excellence, if there is anything worthy of praise, think continually on these things [center your mind on them, and implant them in your heart].*

You need to listen because even when you are walking out of our house in a rush in the morning, and somebody almost runs you over, you might want to think "Okay God, what are you trying to tell me?" He is always trying to tell you something.

Stop! Just stop. If you want to listen from God, you MUST stop being in a rush all the time. How do you do that? Stop being late to ALL your meetings or appointments. Nothing drives me crazier than people that show up late to events or meetings. That just drives me crazy. I used to cram last-minute things to feel more productive.

I used to love saying: "I'm just so busy." When in reality that was just an excuse for my lack of trust in God. The busier I was, the more I thought I was in control. How about you? Have you ever done that?

Have you noticed that when you are running late, you are not paying attention to where you are going? You get to places, and you don't even know how you got there because you were moving on autopilot. When you are on autopilot, you are not listening.

The funny this is that you would still say things like: "God, speak to me; God, please talk to me."

God would, in turn, say something like:

"Really? When am I going to talk to you? Really? When? You ain't never listening. You are NEVER available. You are ALWAYS talking to people; you are always doing something, and you want me to speak to you? You know that I'm a Gentleman. I'm not going to push my way into your life. I'm not going to do that. I am waiting for you to give me an opportunity to come into my presence and say: Daddy, I'm here. Speak to me.'"

Isn't that sad? Do you ever just want to speak to Him? And not because there's nothing happening on Facebook, Twitter or Instagram, or because you don't have something better to do. But because you desire to listen from Him. You need it! You crave it like you crave a good piece of chocolate or meat, vegetables, shoes, bags or whatever. You crave it like it's air.

Have you ever not been able to breathe? Like when you drink, and the water goes down the wrong pipe; your lungs ache, but then after coughing as if your life depended on it, you can inhale sweet oxygen again. You know how good that feels?

God needs to feel that good to you, better than air. That's why you need to listen. Stop being so busy! You are NOT that important.

Your world is not going to end if you don't attend every single event you get invited to. The world is not going to end if you don't comment on every single little post on social media. You need down time. You need it. If you were honest with yourself, you would have to admit: "I need down time."

Next time you go to church, or next time you sit down to pray and you your mind begins to attack you just remember my name. If you cannot pray because too many thoughts are coming at you, you are robbing God of His time.

You may think you are praying, but what you are doing is writing down your to-do list. I can picture God saying: "I'm just going to wait until you finish writing your little to-do list."

Let's face it; you give Him so little time anyway; don't rob Him of that too. Maybe, just perhaps, that's why He's not talking to you as often as you would like Him too.

What is self-care?

Have you heard of it before, right? The phrase has become very popular lately, especially among spas and retreat centers but what is self-care according to God?

You remember back in Genesis chapter 1 and the beginning of chapter 2 when God spoke the world into existence? If you have not read it in a while, please go back and read it when you have a chance. Do it now and come back here afterward.

Fantastic, right? How God created everything; in the correct order and correctly the first time around? Every day He took the time to see what He created and enjoyed it. When He was finished, He rested.

Do you do that? Do you do the work that needs to be done and enjoy it or do you run from one thing to the next without even enjoying it? I can tell you that I was in the habit of doing that. Always doing and always on the move. I would completely miss blessings God had prepared for me because I did not know how to rest. I thought if I kept going and going I would accomplish more but in reality, all I was doing was getting burned out.

If God, the creator of the universe took the time to enjoy His creation and then when all was done rested, then who are we to think we don't need to do the same? As it says in Genesis 1: 26a

A Match Made in Heaven

Then God said, "Let Us (Father, Son, Holy Spirit) make man in Our image, according to Our likeness [not physical, but a spiritual personality and moral likeness];

We are created in His image, so we are to act as He acts. When was the last time you rested?

If you have to think about it for more than a minute, it has been too long.

I want you to take five to ten minutes and think of 10-ways you can incorporate rest into your everyday life: (reading a fun book, going for a walk, a nap, chatting with a friend, a massage, playing a board game, etc. You get the idea.

1._____
_____
2._____
_____
3._____
_____

4._____

_____

5._____

_____

6._____

_____

7._____

_____

8._____

_____

9._____

_____

10._____

_____

How does that feel? Which restful activity will you start doing right away? Circle it above and add it to your calendar.

Chapter Five
Embrace All Outcomes - NOT Everything is About You

Embrace All Outcomes - NOT Everything is About You

Do not let the shame of "what they may think or say" stop you from sharing and accepting that what has happened and is happening is not a surprise to God. And not everything is about you - remember that God is the ultimate recycler. There are so many things happening for you in this season, and then you have the audacity to want to keep all that to yourself?

You have gone through some serious stuff; God has delivered you from things you probably should not have survived for you to say:

"I'm just going to keep this one to myself."

Picture this, in a corner, there is somebody praying: "God, please send me someone that will tell me how they handled this challenge." I am praying for someone who will tell me how You showed up when they needed You the most." While on the other side of the world you have decided to be selfish with your pain.

You might even fool yourself into thinking that you are kind or even humble. "Everything is good; God loves me. Everything is great; I'm on cloud nine." But inside you are dying, and worse yet, you are keeping that to yourself.

Guess what somebody just prayed that very morning for real: "I'm just so tired of people saying that everything is great all the time. Where are the REAL people?" You and I both know that is not possible for EVERYTHING to always great. If that is the case, you are not doing something with your life or your gifts.

If nobody is attacking you, you are not doing anything. If people are not against you at least sometimes, you are not doing anything. If everybody loves you all the time, you are not doing anything. If nothing is happening to you, you might as well be dead. Maybe nobody told you that you were dead. Maybe nobody told you, and you died a long time ago because everything is wonderful all of the time.

Have you ever stop to think that you might be sitting on somebody's blessing including someone's deliverance? How much longer are you going to do that? People are waiting to hear the ugly.

I get it, you want to have your hair done, your nails, and look cute and put together before you start sharing what God has done in your life.

While there is a person in the corner dying, or they are pouring their heart and their soul to God in prayer: "God, send me somebody."

I believe the Holy Spirit ministers to our hearts, but sometimes, we need a flesh and blood person. You need someone in the flesh to tell you, "I know what you are going through and I've been there, but when God showed up, He did come, and He came through for me, and He will do it for you too." When that person hears that, they will get up, wash their face and glorify God and say "God, thank you, for answering my prayers."

God uses people, real people. And you may ask "God, use me. God, give me something, something good." You may want to make more money, a better job or a better car. Those seem to be the testimonies people love to share.

But what about the other stuff? You don't want to tell people about the times you had a problem with eating or gambling. You don't want to tell people that. You don't want to say to them that God delivered you from that problem. You don't want to tell them about your pornography problem either.

You don't want to talk about that because that doesn't deserve the glory? Really? Did not He deliver you from that as well? That deserves glory too. It is not about you. All that stuff that happened, somebody needs it. Someone needs to hear that too - the ugly has value and you keep sitting on it because you are afraid of what they might say or think. That is the truth.

Let's be practical for a minute, think about one of the areas you used to struggle with, pornography for example. Maybe it had a stronghold in your life, and you wanted to stop watching that stuff but as much as you tried you could not. You prayed and even fasted but nothing.

Imagine yourself picking up a book from someone that struggled with that SAME sin for a LONG time but by the grace of God was free from it. Would you read that book? Would you be scouring through the book looking for better understanding of the problem and hoping to find how they were able to break free? You would, right? Well, there are thousands if not millions of people that struggle with the SAME issue(s) you struggle with, and they need you. They need to read about your nights of despair when you cried out for help hoping someone would help you.

See, it is not about you; God wants to use you, warts and all. The books that have blessed me the most are the books that keep it real. The ones that don't sugar coat things or pretend their struggle was not nasty. You know I am speaking truth right now. Get over yourself. IT IS NOT ABOUT YOU!!!

The bad and the ugly

Let's get real, are you ready? Remember, no one can see this book or what you write in it. Is it your safe place to share okay?

Write down below the sin that used to torment you the most:

_____
_____
_____
_____

How do you feel now that you are free from it?

_____

_____

_____

_____

_____

_____

How long did you struggle with that?

_____

_____

Now, what if you had had help from someone that used to struggle with the same issue? How long do you think you would have had to suffer through that?

_____

_____

_____

_____

Knowing what you know now, would not you want to be that for somebody else? Would not you want to end someone else's suffering early instead of prolonging it? Remember you know their pain.

_____

_____

Make a quick list of all the things you learned when God freed you from that stronghold/sin. Things that would help someone else leave sooner than you did.

_____

_____

_____

_____

_____

Be honest, seeing all you have learned because of what you went through would you say it was worth it and why?

A Match Made in Heaven

Chapter Six
Opposition Does Not Mean You Are Going the Wrong Way

Many will try to discourage you and tell you to give up; they will even say: "it's taking too long." They mean well, but they just don't know the inner work God has to do with you before the blessings and promises to come to pass. The reality is that it is taking as long as it's going to take for you to stop fighting God.

I know a thing or two about waiting for His promises. I have known about my calling for a couple of years now. I was so excited too. He said it so I thought the promises would come to pass right away. Silly Catherine. Little did I know about the overhauls my heart and soul need to go through. I did know this: He is worth EVERYTHING, and He who promised is faithful.

With time I learned to listen to what He was saying and the people He was using to guide me and take me to the place I was supposed to be.

I probably should not say this but I will anyway. I wish someone told me to be honest. It would not have deterred me, but it would have better prepared me for the battles. So yes, I must say. Many people are going to come after you. Especially when you are doing EXACTLY what God told you to do.

Many people will come out nowhere like ants after a picnic, and you might be tempted to say:

"Maybe they're right. I mean, maybe I didn't hear from God. Maybe they're right."

They are relentless too; sometimes it's people from your church. They will tell you things like:

"Listen, just stay in your lane. Just do what you are supposed to do."

"Girl, you are too busy, you are everywhere."

"I don't know about that whole Jesus thing."

It is entirely reasonable for you to think: "Well, maybe they're right. Maybe I'm just making this about me."

BUT you know what He said. You know your heart; you know it's not about you. You know that. You know your heart; you know that eventually, the promises will come to pass.

Okay, that was a total bummer, I know. But it had to be said. Ready for some good news? Here it comes: the opposition, most of the time, is telling you that you are going the right way.

You know what happens to your opponent? They know you are going the right way, but at the same time, they know they are being left behind. They know they are not coming with you to the next season. So, what they are trying to do is secure more time with you, but they don't have the guts to say that. They don't have the guts to say,

"I just don't want to be left behind." However, they don't want to change either.

Use the script next time they come at you:

"Opposition, thank you. Thank you for fueling my ministry. Opposition, thank you for letting me know that God is doing amazing things. Opposition, thank you for the confirmation.

Opposition, you are right on track. Keep doing your job; I'm going to do my job. I know what God has called me to do. So, thank you. You know what? You don't even annoy me anymore. You don't steal my peace anymore because I am aware you are just doing your job. Oh my God! You get an A+; you get a sticker, you get a medal, you get something because you are doing exactly what you are supposed to be doing in my life.

However, I will do exactly what God told me to do. You get your medal; I'll get my crown.

When you make up your mind; when you figured out that you are going to quit that job, then come this way. I'll be here. In the meantime, just do what you are supposed to do, but I'm going to keep doing what I'm doing because that's what God told me to do. Nothing else and nothing more. Opposition, thank you, but I'm busy. I got things to do; I got people to see, I got people to deliver. Thank you, opposition. Thank you, but I'm good."

Is not that awesome? You can steal or borrow that script and use it verbatim next time you feel the mutiny of opposition running your way.

Opposition comes in many shapes and forms

The third thing I wish a woman or man of God told me when I started to walk out my calling is that opposition will show up in many forms, not just people or circumstances.

When I stepped out on social media back in 2015 I was so sure of how to use my gifts and talents; it was easy. I loved being on camera and sharing with people, but then it became hard. No warning or heads up. I just could not do it like before.

I would try to do faith-based scopes only and then style-based scopes only, but it just would not work. My fellow business owners would advise me and push me towards keeping everything separate. To be honest at the time that felt like the right thing to do but inside, deep down I knew it was not right.

However, I did not have a precedent, I did not know where to turn for advice. The struggle made me question the calling and even the gifting. Today I know it was opposition. When you decide to step out in faith be on the lookout for people, circumstances, lack, and hardship.

But please remember, it is part of the process. I would not be able to write about it today if I had not gone through it.

Want to know what opposition looks like in your own life/ministry? Take ten-minutes and list the things you are struggling with right now. (Don't leave anything out. No matter how small or insignificant it feels to you. If it makes your life or ministry difficult write it down:

_____
_____
_____
_____
_____
_____
_____
_____
_____
_____
_____
_____
_____
_____
_____

A Match Made in Heaven

_____

_____

_____

_____

_____

_____

_____

_____

_____

_____

Ready to write your own anti-opposition script? I mean mine is pretty good but let's face it that's not how you speak. The script will be more powerful when you make it your own. Read my script again for inspiration and then pray for the Holy Spirit to give you the right words:

_____

_____

A Match Made in Heaven

A Match Made in Heaven

A Match Made in Heaven

_____

_____

_____

_____

_____

_____

_____

_____

_____

_____

Congratulations you now have your very own weapon against those pesky oppositions.

Remember opposition is not to be taken personally or to let waste your time engaging and defending your calling. God called you. Period. No need to waste your precious time explaining to mere mortals what requires a heavenly-minded heart.

Little children (believers, dear ones), you are of God, and you belong to Him and have [already] overcome them [the agents of the antichrist]; because He who is in you is greater than he (Satan) who is in the world [of sinful mankind].

1 John 4:4 AMP

Chapter Seven
Inventory Time: Put The Puzzle Together

Look at that a big old picture. With the little things that we talked about in chapter 1, all the things that have happened to you, I want you to start putting the pieces together - all of the pieces; not just the beautiful ones you think make sense and go together. All the oddly shaped pieces that stand out like Yankee fan at Fenway Park on opening day.

I want you to start playing with them pieces because you have to look at them, you have to put on your Picasso's eyes, and you have to look at them creatively. God allowed all those things to happen. By now you must realize they go together- all of them. Look at them differently. You have to ask for the Holy Spirit to help you. "Holy Spirit, show me what this puzzle is supposed to look like."

It's not going to make sense to anybody else, but it should make sense to you. You don't even know how to work with puzzles because you have natural eyes. The only way to see it all is by putting on our spiritual eyes.

You are not in the natural. That's just for the regular folks. We ain't ordinary. We're different; we're special. Our puzzle is special. It requires a different kind of sight. It requires different eyes. And that's why it doesn't make sense to them. They don't get it. They even say:

"You don't even know what you are doing."

Just tell to not worry about it. He's got it. Tell them that when they change their mind; when they modify the way, they are looking at things, it'll make sense then.

I know this may sound foreign to you so I will give you an example and then you can work on your puzzle.

A Match Made in Heaven

Here are my pieces of my puzzle:

Anointed	Quiet
Divorced	Rejected
Hard working	Rules follower
Leader	Shy
Mother	Special
Non-confrontational	Stubborn
Play-it-safe	Traditional
Preacher's kid	

At first glance, those pieces may seem random to you, but they are not. Some of those pieces might scream disqualified to you, but God had other plans. Let's dig deeper, shall we?

Get a regular job and make lots of money	Ministry is not for me
Gifts of the spirit were meant to stay in the new testament	My way or the highway
	No drama, please
	No Patience

A Match Made in Heaven

People are too
complicated
Women don't preach

Writing at that level will
never take place again

Do you know what God had to do? He had to rewire/refurbish my mind and heart so I would let go of ALL the things I learned and was taught as a child. I had to let go of the limitations put on me by others and myself.

I had to see the calling in others, learn to appreciate it and love it so then and only then I could see my calling. NEVER in a million years did I imagine God would call me to preach or teach others.

The gifts of the spirit were not part of my extensive vocabulary. Words like limits and can't had to be removed and retired from my mind and heart. My puzzle had many pieces that to the naked eye did not add up to who I am today. But I thank my Father for having the patience to mold, prune and shape me into who I am today. The pieces not only fit but went together ever so beautifully; I just needed an eyesight adjustment.

Wow, that was hard to write but so true. Puzzles stop being hard and become fun when we open our mind's to the endless possibilities God has for us.

How about you, what does your puzzle say about you? Pray first, asking God to reveal all the pieces you think don't fit it. Then write. Don't leave any out. Remember, no one can read this book by you, so don't hold back.

_____

_____

_____

_____

_____

_____

_____

A Match Made in Heaven

_____
_____
_____
_____
_____
_____
_____
_____
_____
_____
_____
_____
_____
_____

How was that, hard? I know it was. But in a little bit you will see how it comes together ever so beautifully.

Now let us dig a little deeper. What are those attitudes, circumstances, mistakes, and life experiences that partially or completely contradict what God is saying about you?

You are doing so well. I am SO very proud of you. You are so close to seeing God's masterpiece. Please don't quit now. You are almost there.

Pray again, look at what you wrote and write down: what do you think? Can you see how God orchestrated every wrong and right turn so you could collect EVERY experience, lesson, and scar you would need for your calling? (Don't rush this part, take your time, and make sure you are in a place where you can be honest and the tears can flow freely).

_____
_____
_____
_____
_____
_____
_____
_____
_____
_____

A Match Made in Heaven

How does that feel, amazing and overwhelming at the same time? Then you are feeling exactly what you need to be feeling right now. Wait till you get to chapter 8. Get ready to get your Sunday's best 'cause a wedding is about to go down.

You did awesomely; I am very proud of you. I know God is too.

Chapter Eight
Time to Get Married: Vocation and Calling

It's time to marry your vocation to your calling. Did you know that your calling and your vocation are a perfect match? You no longer have to keep them separate. But before I run ahead of myself, let us define what each of those terms means. Both definitions were taken from The American Heritage College Dictionary, 2007 edition.

Vocation:

A regular occupation, esp. one for which a person is particularly suited or qualified.

Calling:

An inner urge or a strong impulse, esp. one believed to be divinely inspired.

A Match Made in Heaven

More than likely (unless you are one of the blessed ones) you have spent most of your life in your vocation. Doing honest work for pay. There's nothing wrong with that. I shared earlier in the book that I spent seventeen years working in corporate America. However, I just knew there was something else for me, something bigger than myself. Corporate America was the stepping-stone God used to teach me many of the tools I would need in my calling.

We spent seven chapters working and getting ready for this. It is not in our nature to just accept going against the grain. I did not want to rush you. Just like couples should not rush into marriage, God wants us to arrive at the altar of our calling when we are finally ready to make a full commitment to Him.

I was not ready before; I thought I was, but I was not. I did not understand the price required for my calling or the commitment it called for. There were many nights spent in despair, countless tears; fear would come and leave me shattered and hopeless more times I care to count. My faith was tested over and over again until it was not a sad utterance anymore but strong legs and feet that moved mountains.

My prayer life or lack there-of got a massive makeover too. I learned to speak to my Daddy first out of necessity, out of desperation and then out of love and reverence.

My relationships changed too, they became healthy, holy, a source of joy and drove me closer to my Father.

Today, I am no longer afraid to arrive at the altar, with my offerings, gifts, and talents. Still not perfect but understanding that the One that is perfect is in me and has already fulfilled that requirement for me.

I now realize that my vocation and my calling belong together and will no longer be apart.

Remember that prophecy that was given to me back in December? Apostle Louis Jones said something to me, but I didn't get it. I didn't get mad, but I didn't get it. This is what he said:

"Catherine, you have plateaued concerning book writing." I heard those words and immediately thought:

"What are you talking about Willis? What? Me, plateaued?" But I did not have much time to think about the absurdity of the statement because he went on:

"some people will want to work with you because of your anointing, and there is going to be a contract that is coming."

It was like one of those compliments you receive, but after you digest them you are left wondering: "was that even a compliment? Did he just say what he just said?"

The word was given, I sat on it, but I didn't know what he meant by it because I was still writing and the books were still coming. The words were still coming, the titles

A Match Made in Heaven

kept coming, and the anointing was flowing. When I write, I don't get stuck, ever.

Yes, you read that right: I never get writer's block. So, when apostle said that I plateaued, I could not understand what he was talking about because I didn't think I had. But then something happened. I was getting ready to teach a very successful class I had.

I'm a great teacher, by the way. I'm gifted. I did not know that about me. I am not bragging on myself; I am just surprised at how God can use someone like me to teach others. Anyway, I found out I could teach by mistake.

Somebody tried to dissuade me, to discourage me from teaching. Now let me tell you a little something about me when someone pushes me I push back. I know that I may look small, but I'm strong. So, if someone tells me that I cannot do something it fuels my type-A, competitive, my lets-get-this-thing-done-button gets activated, and my brain is in all-systems-go mode.

A Match Made in Heaven

I took teaching on almost as a dare or a challenge. I did not count on totally and utterly falling in love with it. I LOVE teaching. I can do it all day long. But I digress, back to the story, so I pushed the class. I mean I pushed HARD, and nothing happened.

I talked to people, nothing happened. I made the class even better; like ridiculously awesome. I went above and beyond. Not a single enrollment.

The not so funny thing was that I couldn't push it the way I pushed before because I didn't feel I had the freedom to. Can you believe I had hit a plateau and I didn't even know it? Did I give up? Nope. I kept pushing because I'm a worker. As I continued to struggle I finally had to ask Him:

"God, what is it? Is it a ministry? Is it a business? I don't think I want to do business; I just want to do ministry. What do I do?"

And I kept asking because I didn't know which way to go; I thought I had to choose one or the other. I remembered something I used to say during my Livestream intros:

"I can do all those things at the same time because I don't have to and I don't want to choose."

God is so amazing; do you know what He did? He narrowed the things I used to do; He narrowed my focus. To this day, He keeps narrowing things down for me. I found myself telling Him:

"God, what do I do? I don't like to plateau; I like to go up and up and up."

That is how I am! I don't know about you, but I know there is no limit to the things I can do in Jesus Christ? There is no limit!

I have also found that when we ask God the right questions, He answers quickly. What did he do? He brought me to Philippians 4. Just like you, I was VERY familiar with Philippians 4 Already. My point is that I could not understand why God was bringing me to that scripture but I would soon find out.

I am a very independent woman. I am self-sufficient because God made me that way. I told Him:

"God, I'm not what I am supposed to be. I'm meant to be dependent, but I don't know how to do that. Can you please show me how?"

And then He showed me why He took me to Philippians 4:13 AMP

*I can do all things [which He has called me to do] through Him who strengthens and empowers me [to fulfill His purpose—**I am self-sufficient in Christ's sufficiency;** I am ready for anything and equal to anything through Him who infuses me with inner strength and confident peace.]*

Paul said: "I am sufficient in Christ's sufficiency."

A Match Made in Heaven

God did not make a mistake when He created me. I am supposed to be self-sufficient as long as I am self-sufficient in Christ's sufficiency. That was the part I was missing. There is nothing wrong with me. There' is nothing wrong with the way He created me. I am supposed to be self-sufficient as long as I'm going to the source, as long as I'm relying on His sufficiency for my life.

So, when God revealed my calling to me, and I was able to see it, FINALLY I said:

"Yes, I will marry my vocation to my divine calling."

Let's put it all back together by going back to the prophecy.

"Catherine, people are going to call you, you are going to get a contract; you have plateaued regarding the book writing."

God was speaking about a new level in Him; I just couldn't see it.

A Match Made in Heaven

God said to me:

"Catherine, you are a ghostwriter. You are going to be working with leaders one on one, faith-based leaders and lay professional leaders. You are going to help them, one on one, to write their books, whether they are going to learn for themselves or they want you to ghostwrite their book for them."

All I could muster was: "What, me?"

Did you know what happened almost immediately? Three people asked me to ghostwrite their book for them, and I just could not receive it or see it.

Have you ever been there, where someone recognizes who you are before you do? Well, it happened to me. Ever since God revealed that to me I have been having next-level conversations about ghostwriting and other projects. And to think that everything started with the word: plateau.

A Match Made in Heaven

Everything I had learned when I used to be a personal stylist I can now bring to a book, like bringing more essence/authenticity.

My corporate career taught me how to be analytical and figure out how much to charge my clients and students. I'm supposed to have a business; I get to work with faith-based leaders and lay professionals too.

Do you now see why I had to plateau and get to the end of myself so I can see the next level? Or why my class was not working anymore? It worked before; it just doesn't work for the level God promoted me to.

I gave as much as I needed to give in that class but I was holding on to it because I loved that class. But God was saying:

"Honey, I'm taking you to a new level."

Do you see why I have to get married now? That was a long story I know, but I needed to bring you to this point, to your story. This book is not about my story but YOURS.

A Match Made in Heaven

Where do your vocation and your Divine calling collide? Write below what it means to marry your vocation to you calling. Don't forget to ask the Holy Spirit for guidance and clarity.

_____

_____

_____

_____

_____

_____

_____

_____

_____

_____

_____

_____

_____

A Match Made in Heaven

A Match Made in Heaven

Chapter Nine
Why It Took So Long To See

Do you understand why it took so long to see your development and why your other endeavors did not work? I remember applying to a big program awhile back, but my application was rejected. I wondered, why I denied. I was going to have to spend six months with them in training, but God said:

"Honey, you are already trained. You don't need to go through any more training. You are done, you are done." It was not a denial. Darling, you are beyond that. Why are you asking them to train you when I already did it? I already did it, so the denial is nothing but deliverance.

Let me ask you, what is God saying to you? Could it be:

"Honey please, no more school. You are done. No more, you are done. I trained you; you are good. Whatever denial you just received, whatever doors I just closed on your nose is because you have arrived at the right place already."

You couldn't handle the marriage before, and that's why God delayed the union until you could take care of it; until you could become the person who could not only handle it but could thrive in it.

Why it took so long, why could not we arrive at this realization until this chapter? So, you could marry the right vocation to the right divine calling. So, you could become the chosen person and FINALLY say:

 "I'm ready. I'm here. I can do it all as long as I delight in my sufficiency in Christ."

Guess what? I no longer push a halved car. I put the car together, and now I got in the car, and I'm zipping through as I was always meant to do. I'm going fast because I said yes to the right marriage. I was able to put my puzzle together. The picture makes sense. What are you going to do with what you have learned? Are you ready for your marriage?

Write below ALL God has revealed to you thus far, about yourself, your calling, your past and your future:

_____
_____
_____
_____
_____
_____
_____
_____
_____
_____
_____
_____

A Match Made in Heaven

A Match Made in Heaven

Chapter Ten
And This is Why I Write….

My calling, my divine calling is not only to write books like this one but to teach others how to do it for themselves. Writing is the vehicle God used in my life to heal me and to show me who I was in Him. And writing is the vehicle God wants me to use in my divine calling.

Can you believe it? The thing that first brought me so much joy and happiness but then lost. He brought it back, but not at the level I used to have but much better. Improved and upgraded.

When we lose something, we are meant to have while pursuing God He will bring it back but not the at the same level. While we are searching, growing and becoming Who He created us to be He is also enlarging the territory and capacity of the gift.

The more I use my gift of writing the more it grows. The more He blows my mind with it and through it. For example, when I'm teaching, and I have to explain something to a student or a client the Holy Spirit drops it in my spirit in the simplest of ways and always on time.

I keep the list of books I want to write and ideas on my Evernote app so I can access it whether I am working on my beloved MacBook Pro or my iPhone. Can I tell you that the ideas never stop coming? The books just flow, I could be walking or eating, and it would just hit me.

Just like when I was a young girl, and I would have to get up in the middle of the night, find a notebook quickly so I could jot down whatever inspiration the Holy Spirit shared with me (I just did not it was Him speaking to me then), but now the ideas are bigger and more anointed.

I write books because I cannot keep to myself the wonders my Daddy keeps doing around and in my life. Books are my way of sharing with the world how awesome God is and how He is the only one that can take a broken and messed up person and turned them into a beautiful vessel for His glory.

I write because I have been redeemed, I have been made new and because I wish someone had told me before that it was possible. I wish there were a book my younger self could have read that said:

"Yes, God wants to use you. He is calling you not in spite of your past and transgressions but because of them. He delights in using the foolish things of this world so all can see Who He is. So, EVERY knee would bow and recognize that only He can knit together the perfect amount of brokenness and turn it into something so beautiful that others must turn to Him."

Writing is my vehicle, the gift given to me so I could glorify God and share with you, and the world what He has done in my life. What is your vehicle, what is your gift?

_____
_____
_____
_____

Conclusion

You are now married. Congratulations! Or Good wishes.

Now, the real work begins and be of good cheer because it's not going to be hard. You are in the right place. You are wearing the right shoes; you have the right outfit on, you have the right connections; you have the right degree. You don't have to push or force things anymore.

You have to tell the right people, the ones assigned to you. You got to leave some things behind. When you get married, you don't have relationships like you used to have. You no longer use Facebook Messenger or texting the way you used to before. You don't go to places you used to go before because now you are married.

A Match Made in Heaven

Some things have to be left behind, there are some things that need to stop, there are some people that cannot come with you into your next season, and that's part of the marriage.

When you are married for real, for real, for real, you realize who you are, and you assume your new name. That's when you are born again when you finally accept your divine calling. You are born again. You have a new name, not only that, but you are married now.

You are married now the right way. Isn't that amazing? Isn't that worth-changing for? Isn't that worth NOT hiding anymore? You have been hiding. Brides don't hide. Have you ever seen a hiding bride?

Brides don't hide, they are positioned front and center, and everyone can see them a mile away. You don't even have to ask: "Who is the bride?"

Brides self-identify, they wear the right dress, her hair looks the right way, her makeup is fitting for the occasion. Everybody can tell she is the bride, no longer a bridesmaid.

You don't even have to tell people; they'll say: "This is who you are. You are a bride."

You are a bride, don't you let anybody tell you otherwise. You have been called for such a time as this.

If you get denied doing what you are supposed to be doing, you are talking to the wrong people. The right people don't say no. The right people say: "Where have you been?"

They do not ask: "how much." They say: "Where have you been?" This is your new day; this is your new season.

When you find yourself in a situation and somebody says no to you early in the process thank him or her.

You got places to go. You have to go to places where people are ready to give you their yesses.

I can only speak for myself, but this is what I am prepared to say in this season: "I'm done, I'm out."

When others ask: "Where is Catherine?" Please tell them that Catherine is gone. Catherine is on her honeymoon, and she takes honeymooning very seriously. Thank you very much.

Some people are going to miss it. If they did not get it while the getting was good, they are going to miss it. Many missed their chance to collaborate or work with me, and I am okay with that.

I gave for a very long time to the wrong people. I am ready to serve the right people now.

A Match Made in Heaven

I'm married. I'm different. I'm happy to be different. I'm glad I don't fit in. Thank you, God. I don't fit in. Thank you, Jesus.

About the Author

I am a writer's teacher/coach, Amazon Best-Selling Author, Keynote/TEDx Speaker, confidence-building creator, and minister. I have been coaching (that includes: organizing/optimizing, shopping and confidence building) others (everything started with the need of finding my authentic style) for more than twenty years (even when I did not know it yet). I never thought my love for words, books, and writing would allow me to pool my expertize and help others to bring out their authentic voice from hiding.

My 12-years of corporate purchasing in multiple industries, strategic sourcing experience, combined with my 6-years of coaching, and writing/teaching give me a well-balanced array of tools and expertize to choose from and generously share when helping others uncover and polish their authentic voice.

Today I get to work with committed faith-based leaders and professional men and women who are willing and ready to serve others in a global capacity. However, they know they need the confidence, guidance, and tools to successfully embraced their authentic voice so they can write impactful and relevant books.

Let's connect online:

Facebook: https://www.facebook.com/WritingMadeSimple4Me/
Instagram: https://www.instagram.com/writingmadesimple/
YouTube: http://bit.ly/confidenceTV
Twitter: https://twitter.com/CatStoring
Website: http://writingmadesimple.today/

I have a FREE gift for you. I recorded a Master Class JUST for you! This Master Class will help you not only to find your calling but to also FINALLY accept it.

Request your FREE Master Class here: http://bit.ly/ammihbook-giveaway

My gift to you,

Catherine E. Storing

A Match Made in Heaven

www.ingramcontent.com/pod-product-compliance
Lightning Source LLC
Chambersburg PA
CBHW070459100426
42743CB00010B/1684